Oxford Revision Course

Active Study Skills

ORC publishing

www.oxfordrevisioncourse.com

Colin Murphy

Contents

1 Introduction

A student once asked me, 'why would students bother reading a boring book about study skills when they can't be bothered reading their textbooks?' They have a good point. So, to offer a solution to this I have attempted to produce a short, easy to navigate book which focuses on active and practical ways that you can improve your study skills, revision and exam technique.

The techniques I mention in this book are not magic; they will work if you work at using them. But the responsibility is on you to be an **active learner**. You don't get the top grades by sitting around playing games or watching stuff on your laptop. You need to work at it, that is, work at *study*. You need to put effort into succeeding. Mike Evans, in his book *How to Pass Every Exam* put it like this:

> *'If you don't do much work throughout the year and do very little revision then you will probably fail, and you deserve to.'*

What I want to share are the techniques that help you improve your active study skills, the techniques that get you through your exams and the academic year. I teach study skills and test out these ideas on my students and myself. I have included here the techniques and tips that have produced the best results. If you are willing to use them.

I am going to keep it as short as I can.

A little bit about my background...

I teach and have studied Psychology. I was fortunate to have a lecturer at university called Prof. Aidan Moran. He published a book the year I started called *Managing your Learning at University*. The book used psychological techniques and research to explain how learning worked and also gave you step-by-step techniques to improve your study. I found it really helpful and it has a strong influence on this book. When I began teaching Psychology to students in the UK, I introduced the study skills techniques into my classroom and it had positive results. It was years later that I became a study skills co-ordinator in a college and helped students with problems studying.

I have learned so much from the different problems students have in relation to study. I believe that I have covered many of these common problems here. I also became very interested in making study less boring, by encouraging students in being more creative in how they approach study. This is something we deal with later in the book. Study should not be boring – if it is, you need to look at ways of making it more interesting.

I hope you don't find this book too boring, I have read so many study skills books that, while meaning to be useful, can seem quite dull or pitched at the wrong audience. At the heart of it is this: study skills books are a list of things to do and solutions to problems of study. Reading them and doing nothing is a complete waste of time.

Just a quick task for you to do: **grab a piece of paper and write down what you think your problems with study are**. Have you done it? If you have, well done. If not, are you aware of what problems you have? You need to actively try these techniques out and see if they solve your problems. I force my students to make this list and then show them the techniques that overcome the problems. It could be a list as mundane as time management, concentration, dealing with distractions or just worry and anxiety. Once you come up with a list of things that concern your ability to study you can start finding solutions and then use them. Notice how I put the text in bold in the paragraph above? I'll do this for key ideas and activities throughout the book for those of you who want to quickly draw out the key points from each chapter.

Each chapter ends with a summary, just in case you want to be reminded of the key details of the chapter, and mainly because some of the techniques are easy and need to be done in order to become an effective student.

About Oxford Revision Course

Oxford Revision Course was set up to offer high quality and accessible education to as wide a group as possible, using the best tutors and running a series of courses for English-speaking and international students. Oxford Revision Course guides are designed to share the skills of these tutors to as large a group of people as we can. They also link to top quality courses that help students achieve the best results. The guides are designed to be short and affordable.

2 Time management

This chapter is all about time management, procrastination and a little about motivation. The truth is that motivation usually comes from action. We all know this. We sit around feeling annoyed because we have work to do and get stressed. But as soon as we start doing something, we feel that it is not as difficult, sometimes we even feel a little better. It is often the starting that is difficult. I say to my students, if you have time to think about studying then you have time to study, you just need to plan and organise yourself. According to Butler and Hope:

> '*A survey of students showed that the main difference between good students and average students was in the ability to get down to work quickly. The first tool of time management is to get to the task at hand. Do not spend time in that limbo of neither getting down to the work nor enjoying your leisure.*' If you are reading this book, then I have overcome my procrastination, I have written a book (I had to use my own advice to do it).

Time management is something that many people have issues with, not just students. In working life it can be just as devastating when people fail to manage their time. It can be more devastating in terms of employability if people act like some students do. With some simple ideas here I hope they help you take control of your study.

So how much time should you spend studying? The best answer to this is about **40–50 minute chunks**, not a day but at a time. You should then take a break and come back, but the break should not last longer than the study session, which is often exactly what happens. A good idea is to sit down beforehand and **make a list of what you need to do**.

Make a record of your week

One task I ask my students to do is to record what they do with their time. I asked the students to **account for 24 hrs a day, seven days a week in one-hour slots using a blank timetable**. This is simple and something I suggest you do now.

When a student comes to me with issues with study, I ask them how they use their time. They are sometimes aware of how they use their time but mostly they aren't great at remembering or they don't want to admit how much time they waste. This task, while being simple, can be difficult to get some students to complete. They know they are being ineffective at time management, will admit to having done no real work that week but still won't record what they have done. Some will try to fill it in just before they see me, or have whole days missing. I have concerns about how effective my help will be if they refuse to record their activities for a week.

So as I have stated, I advise you to do this task. Record for a week what you do; every last detail. How many hours are spent watching TV, travelling, or on the phone? If you are spending hours on your phone, make a note of what you are doing. Then make changes – they might be just tiny adjustments that get you back in control. If you are spending three hours a day watching YouTube, maybe reduce this by 2 hours and 45 minutes.The process of recording your actions over a week means you can start to make adjustments and take control of your time. We will always have something more interesting to do than study and this is because students give themselves choices. Find out what recurring pattern of time mismanagement you have. Study should be important for you, so you should choose to study. That is if you want to do well in your exams. If not, don't. It is, after all, your choice.

Record the dates when topics have been covered

I encourage my students to keep a close eye on how long they have spent on each of their subjects, units, etc. **Write down the dates when you covered a topic – you could use a big sheet of paper for this**. You are then aware of the last time you covered the material and for how long. This helps you when it comes to revision. We have already mentioned that we like doing what we like doing. So we will spend more time on a topic we like and enjoy, but this can cause problems when it comes to exams. So, by recording what you have done for each unit/subject and when you have done it, you can have a better understanding of how you have used your time in relation to all your topics.

This simple technique is very effective and could save your skin. Students will think they have covered something well, when in fact they have not looked at the topic in over six months. This could mean that they have completely forgotten what they have covered. Memory is unreliable and if you can remember everything that you have done then you have either some sort of fascinating brain abnormality or you have done nothing at all. As time passes, you may feel you have covered the material but you only *recognise* it and don't actually *remember* it. So, keeping a record of what you have covered is very useful and will help you later on. Some people really don't want to do this but if you are disorganised and frequently take days off where you do nothing, then this habit will help you remember what you have done and, more importantly, what you have *not* done.

Wasting time on the internet

Students at the University of Pennsylvania were able to study wasting time on the internet as an elective course from 2015 onwards. So if you want to continue wasting your time on the internet then this may be the course for you. The course was being offered by the University's Department of English to students with an English or Creative Writing major, and was being run by Professor Kenneth Goldsmith. According to the University's website, its aims were a little more creative. Here is the blurb:

'We spend our lives in front of screens, mostly wasting time: checking social media, watching cat videos, chatting, and shopping. What if these activities — clicking, SMSing, status-updating, and random surfing — were used as raw material for creating compelling and emotional works of literature? Could we reconstruct our autobiography using only Facebook? Could we write a great novella by plundering our Twitter feed? Could we reframe the internet as the greatest poem ever written? Using our laptops and a wifi connection as our only materials, this class will focus on the alchemical recuperation of aimless surfing into substantial works of literature.' My quick answer to the question to all those possibilities is 'probably not'. Give it a go, it may interest some of the students reading this book for a moment. The internet is awesome, watching cat videos can be fun. The question is, are we wasting too much time doing nothing and watching others do nothing? Even more important, is it stopping students from getting better grades?

Communications regulator Ofcom said UK adults spend an average of eight hours and 41 minutes a day on media devices, compared with the average night's sleep of eight hours and 21 minutes. Okay, so it is only 20 minutes more, but if you are someone who doesn't get much sleep then it could be so much more time. A quick check of Facebook is never a quick check. You may look at a status, look at some pictures, 'like' a picture or two, try and think of something witty to say, read something from a page you liked, share a stupid video that one of your friends shared, etc. All of this is sort of okay but, if you are neglecting what it is you are supposed to be doing, namely *study*, then this is a poor decision. Every generation has had their own levels of distractions. The books written about time wasting from the past can be as relevant today as they were then. So if you are reading this book and Instagram and Snapchat have fallen out of fashion like Myspace and bebo did. The point still stands – social media can be overused and distracting from your study.

Don't be distracted by your mobile phone

It is probably a good idea to **deal with using mobile phones** when studying now. Lots of students will have their phones beside them when they are studying, some can't even last a whole lesson without looking down at them. The use of twitter, snapchat, WhatsApp and Facebook mean they are constantly within reach of each other. Just Stop.

Ask yourself, how much of this communication is actually important? Don't be afraid of what might happen if you don't answer. Would people really stop liking you? If your friendship is so fragile that you need to constantly be in touch with each other then something somewhere has gone wrong.

Put it on airplane mode, just for the forty minutes that you are studying. Close all the apps. It is only for a short time. The more you get used to this, the better you can use your time in the exam.

People are becoming more addicted to their technology and you will need to exercise control to stop this. You can't be productive and effective if you don't switch it off from time to time. When I mark exams for A levels I switch my phone off so I can focus on the answers and grade them properly. It would be a shame to think I put more effort in to the marking than the student did into learning the material. When I am at work I would love to do nothing, meet with friends, watch movies and TV shows. The truth is I wouldn't have a job for long. I would be cheating my students and their chances to succeed. So hopefully you realise that **your job is to be a student** and this simple idea of beginning to take control of the distractions like smartphones is helpful in making you more productive.

I am not saying *don't* use your smartphones. They are some of the most powerful tools for studying you have at your disposal. **You could put the timer on for 20**

minutes or use the stopwatch to log your study time. You should then **keep a record** of when and for how long you've been working. There are apps that help you keep track of your time.

Study first

Another simple idea is to *not* say 'I can study *or* I can see my friends or go on Instagram'. We have a tendency to choose the other, easier option. If you say to yourself 'I can study or meet with friends', then the friends option wins most of the time. The simple thing to say is 'I am going to study and *then...*'. This changes it for you. When you take the choice of alternatives to study it can create a flood of avoidance strategies.

Every time you say yes to something, you say no to something else. If you say yes to meeting your friends and watching every episode of a TV series, you are saying no to a potential A grade. That is your choice. When you plan your time and take control of the tasks you're supposed to be doing then you can do all the things you want to do, after you have completed your work. All too often I have seen students fail exams or get much lower grades because of this. I once asked as many students as I could following their last exam (I didn't want to stress them out during the exam period), 'if you could do one thing differently for the exams what would it be?' The most consistent statement was they would have started studying earlier.

I am not saying you can't do other things and only study, it is just about making sure you have planned this rather than drifting from day to day. If you are unable to say no to people, it is important that you learn to. It is okay to be selfish for the sake of high grades, within reason of course. If your friends ask you to go out for some beers, or to watch a movie, offer them alternatives so your fear of offending them is reduced; tell them you are busy now and need to finish your work, but if you have it done by the weekend you could go out then. If this sounds alien to you then you need to sort out your priorities.

The best time to study

Another idea that helps you take control of your time is to **consider when you work best**. If you work best in the morning (something that is unlikely with most of the students that I deal with) then plan to work in the morning. If you are the kind of person who works best in the evening then that is when you should be working. Don't plan to go out with your friends in the evening if that is when you work your best. Do your work first and then go out, if you must. If you have bad sleeping patterns, then you will need to adjust these. The earlier you do this the better.

I have looked at over 500 timetables that people have recorded for a week, and when people go out for parties then they can lose up to about two days of work or more. This is fine if you really deserve to do this (a family or birthday event, for instance). If it is a habit that you go out all the time and sacrifice your grades, then that is your choice, but expect the results to reflect this. I will discuss the idea of planning so you *can* actually have time off, but this is something that should be done, as I have said, when you have your work done.

If you have no idea when you work best, test it out at different times. I have found that while I would probably tell you that I work best in the evening, I actually get more done if I get down to it first thing in the morning. That way the usual habits of putting things off, chatting with friends or whatever people do to avoid work can be avoided earlier. If you need to get two hours of work done, an essay prepared or notes made, start earlier and try to get it done. If this sounds too much hassle then you need to think again about what you want from study.

Avoid cramming

I am amazed at how much effort students will try to put in in the last few weeks of the term before exams. They will write numerous essays and make pages and pages of notes. This same amount of effort and hard work earlier on would be better. Because leaving things to the last minute or cramming can be disastrous. Cramming it all in the last few moments of a week or just before the exam is not a good strategy. People always give me anecdotal information about how it worked for them. But when the topic gets tougher or you have lots more to do then **cramming is the least effective strategy you can use**. While an element of rapid revision at the end is unavoidable as you panic and start worrying about the exam, it is important that you do your best to avoid it. The best way to study is to **space the study sessions out** or distribute them throughout the day and throughout the week. Another helpful tip is to also **start with the subjects that you find most boring**. If you do the task you don't want to do first, then you are more likely to do it. When we put off the tasks we dislike until later we will inevitably be more tired and less likely to want to do them. It takes more self-control and commitment to do something that is harder to do when you are tired and bored. So simply do the things that are important and, if you don't like them, you can start with them first. It will increase your effectiveness.

Test yourself every day

Linked to this is something that is really important, which is to **set some time aside each day to test yourself**. Students hate this more than writing notes on things that they find boring. I will suggest it a few times throughout this book so don't fight it, just do it. I once visited the library in our school and a student close to the exams had a sheet of paper he was reading. I left and then returned two hours later and he still had the same sheet of paper. I asked him about it and he replied that he was 'learning it'. I suggested that he test himself. So I took the paper off him and he wrote out what he remembered. He remembered everything but about two points. But had he tested himself to begin with, he might have found that he already knew a lot of the relevant information and saved himself an hour or two.

When students take a passive approach like just reading their notes they create a problem. I call it the **error of recognition**, that is, when they open the books, they recognise the pictures and text. The problem is they don't *know* it, they just *recognise* it. So by testing yourself each day you are more likely to find out whether or not you have actually learned the information.

My advice is to make sure that you have set some time aside to test yourself. I have put this in time management as it is *vital* that you sit down and test yourself. Use flashcards, blank pieces of paper, self-made quizzes etc. I have tested this idea out on my students, when I say 'let's go over...', students will happily say 'we have done it' upon which I will then promptly say 'well then, close your books and write everything you know about this, or more specific questions'. Students will then realise that there are parts missing. If they all perfectly answer it, I move on.

Most of my lessons start or end with my students being tested.

Procrastination

Now is a good time to discuss **procrastination**. Procrastination is putting things off or choosing less urgent tasks to deal with. There are many reasons why we do this. It can be as simple as a lack of self-control or, at its most basic, not putting more effort into it. It could be, as some suggest, a fear of failure: people avoid the task because they think they will not do a good enough job and so it is not worth the effort. This is giving up or avoiding the problem.

A lot of research suggests stress could be the major cause of procrastination. I will deal with that in the chapter on stress. Many procrastinators say they perform better under pressure. This may often just be an excuse; it is more likely that it is poor planning or lack of goals. Some people put things off way past the timeframe that would allow them to do it comfortably or even to the best of their ability. I procrastinate, but if you are reading this book then this is one time I didn't put it off. If I can use the techniques in this book to avoid procrastination then so can you.

There are countless books published on procrastination, so common is this problem. One book is called *The 15 minute rule: How to stop procrastinating and take charge of your life* By Caroline Buchanan. The idea of this is that you **give yourself fifteen minutes to work at the problem, study or task**. It pretty much says it in the title. This is no different to the Pomodoro technique. You **work for 25 minutes, take a break and then work for another 25 minute burst.** These techniques are effective and simple to start using. The key to this is to **form a habit**. You must spend time trying to do it over and over again.

I used these techniques to write this book. I spent the spare time I had in between lessons, missed appointments, while watching something stupid in the evening on TV. I mixed it with the technique I talk about later – having a clear goal. So if you are reading this, then it clearly works or at least I clearly made it work for me.

Do a small part of your task immediately

Much of the quick time management strategies that I mentioned earlier are useful in overcoming the problem of putting things off (e.g. setting time aside every day to test yourself, working in 40–50 minutes chunks, and recording what you've covered). A similar, simple trick to use is to **do a small part of the task as soon as you think about it**. That can be any part of the task. For instance, if you have some homework set on Monday afternoon, set aside a short amount of time to do something on it as soon as your class finishes. Organise the notes you need to make, pick the chapters you want to study and then set a time to do it, create a very basic essay plan, etc.

The rule of five

Another catchy idea is the **rule of five**. Say to yourself that you will do five minutes, five pages or write five paragraphs. The chances are that you will do more but it gets you started. I used this technique to get me started with the editing of this book. I told myself I would do an hour or 2500 words before I had it proofed. I have been here three hours and edited the first 6000 words to this point.

Think of study as a job

Books have been written based on time management strategies, filled with successful case studies of people who put things into action. By all means read them, but know that the key principle is about *you taking action.* So put all of these strategies together and you may get things done.

Be honest with yourself. If you think that you deserve to have holidays during the academic year, that you have some right to finish early, take weekends off or stay out late then how do you expect or feel that you have the right to top grades? This is an inherent flaw in thinking. I see students regularly avoid work, deadlines and study who have no problem organising weekends away with friends or going on holiday. They fail to appreciate that these are things that you could do but only if you have done your work and achieved your results. The brutal honesty is that people who say they will 'study' and then go on holiday, rarely do. Some people can, but if you have not covered the material, not finished your work or study then you are not taking a well-earned break, you are just avoiding the work and need to take control and plan it better. Every course I have taught on has a summer holiday, so do your holidaying then. If you are really into, for instance, skiing, surfing or mountain climbing and it is an essential part of your core being then make sure you have completed everything you need to *before* you go. Payne and Whittaker in *Developing Essential Study Skills* suggest that:

> *'It is a good idea to think of study as a job. It will require a lot of dedication, motivation and commitment to be successful. But, of course, like all jobs, studying can be carried out either effectively and efficiently, or ineffectively and inefficiently. The way to improve study habits is to manage time effectively. ... It is not a good idea to study for all the time available to you; scheduling time off and relaxation activities into your week is important. Similarly, do not go to so many parties and other social activities that you neglect your work, you will be in an appropriate frame of mind for studying and you will be able to enjoy your leisure time with a clear conscience.'*

So do your job with some pride, and if you find your job of study difficult then use these techniques and seek help if you need it. I have worked with some of the best students. The thing that really works is that they seek help very early on, they ask teachers for more work, better materials; they are active in their pursuit of learning.

Task management

One final point to help you with managing your time, this is dealt with later in Chapter 3, but is best put by Andrew Northedge when he said:

> *'Try to balance time management against task management. If you become too obsessed with time, you tend to think in terms of 'hours put in' rather than what you have achieved, then you find yourself "filling up" time with relatively unimportant tasks. To avoid this, you need to set out with the goal of completing specific tasks (even if you don't always succeed). On the other hand, if you focus too much on completing a task you can let it drag on for too long and it will stop you attending to something else just as important. You need to switch your attention between task management and time management to achieve a balance.'*

This advice is important as it keeps you focused and

not just trying to fill time.

SUMMARY

1 Record what you do with your time and make adjustments if necessary.

2 You can do things other than study, just make sure you plan them.

3 Cramming is not the best way to study, it is important to distribute your learning, it has been suggested that 40–50 minutes is as much as you can do without taking a break.

4 Don't let your breaks be longer than your study period.

5 Start with the boring stuff first, you won't want to come back to it later when you are tired.

6 Set some time each day to test yourself, this is so important as it will check to see if you have actually learned anything. If you haven't learned it go back and review it.

7 Don't give yourself choices; you study and then you do the other thing.

8 Use spare moments (like waiting for a bus) to do something that will help you in revision. This is also useful if you are tired. So make flashcards, PowerPoint,

even organise your notes.

9 Be aware of procrastination. If you are putting things off, work on identifying why and what action you can take.

10 Tell yourself you will do 15 minutes work, or five minutes or five pages or 500 words.

11 Record what you have done, this helps you when it comes to revision. It could be that you have avoided a whole topic or not studied something for months.

12 Look at making some plans/goals these help you to work more on a task by breaking it down. Goals are motivational and give you control over your study. This way you can think of balancing between time management and task management.

3 Goals

Completing goals and working towards finishing a goal can be amazing. Goals sound like a dirty word to most students. When I discuss them in class, students tend to shrug their shoulders and ignore them, yet it may be the most important thing in this book. I know, 'Goals' sound like something you would learn from a slick-suited self-help guru. Hear me out though, this *really* works.

Goals help you to avoid procrastination and give you deadlines. They let you know when you have finished a task, or when you are halfway through. They give you control. Goals are, at the very least, motivating. If they are not motivating you then you have not got the right goal or are not tackling it correctly. Goals help you to work more effectively and they give you tasks that you need to do so you can break down more complex ideas or projects into something more manageable. They also reduce stress when used regularly and they even free up some time.

If you only have a vague idea about what you are supposed to be doing, then you will get vague results. You won't really be engaged in the task, you won't know when to start or when to finish. You will have the feeling of a never-ending chore of study, with no true beginning and no end. **Goals will give you control**.

I hope I have sold them well because I know that they do work. When students come to a study skills clinic for help around revision I use variants of goal planning to help them get back on task. To increase the likelihood of you actually completing the goals, it might be a good idea to **reward yourself after you have completed your goal**, or when you have reached the half-way mark.

SMART targets

Goal setting is a process by which we set the targets for ourselves, so you may want to think about what it is you want to do for all of your studies. The core idea is that you **use the SMART technique**. SMART is an acronym credited to both Peter Drucker (1955) and G.T. Doran (1981) which pops up all the time in business and sports.

SMART stands for:

Specific

Measurable

Action-related

Realistic

Time-based

This technique will help you become more effective if used correctly but that doesn't mean you can't adapt it for your own needs. So, let's say your general attitude to study is that you will 'do some biology later', that is far too vague and, well, not very motivating. 'Some biology' could mean anything and most of it would be unrelated to study.

This is where you use the first part of the SMART technique; you become more **specific**; you make your goal or task clearer:

> *'Between nine and ten tonight I am going to make notes on the heart and test myself'*

This is a little more specific and this in itself a little more motivating. The next part is to make it **measurable**. If you don't measure the progress you have made, you could lose interest and allow more interesting things (like chasing your dog or shouting at pigeons) get in the way. So let us say you are writing a book about study skills. You could say that you will do 500 words a day. That is manageable and you can work through this. It reminds you when you keep a record of the amount you have done, it also allows you to see that you are making progress.

The next step is **action-related** and this is where you identify all the parts of the task at the beginning. Each step takes you closer to completion. It also helps you break big goals into more manageable chunks. For example, writing an essay would involve setting time aside to gather the books, read and choose material. Then you can divide up the amount of words you need to do each day and set aside time for the first draft and for rewriting.

The next stage is about being **realistic**. If you have left yourself two days to write a thesis, chances are you aren't going to get it done. Your study goals should be realistic, if you don't get what is realistic and what is not then talk to your teachers, friends and family about what you need to do and work from there. Sometimes a teacher will tell you that it is impossible for people to move up a few grades if you are sitting an exam again. This may drive you to prove them wrong. The truth is, the majority of these advisors will be cautious. It may take a lot of effort and hard work to get the grades. I have worked with students for years who say their goal is to get an A. Yet they do very little work and they get the same results again, they have a Goal 'to get an A' but they have no idea of what steps to take or what they need to do to get it. The students with clear goals and a desire to improve their results mixed with the hard work, tend to do better.

The final step is to make sure that your goal is **time-based**. Using this guide as an example, if I set a target to be 10000 words by the 22nd of November then I have a deadline to work towards. Many people say they work well under pressure. The truth is most of them are ignorant of the deadlines or pressures because they think something is far away. They are not actually working better as they have no idea what it is like to complete a task on time or to the highest standard.

The best thing you can do is to **work backwards from the date the goal should be completed**, to the present day. This task is really good for you to see what needs to be done and when. So let's say you have a textbook with 12 chapters to study and make notes on in the next 12 weeks. Then you can easily divide the task into a chapter a week for the next 12 weeks. I always suggest that students have a halfway mark, so in 6 weeks you have half of it completed. Then, if you get ahead of yourself as some chapters are less complicated, you can feel good about the work you have done.

If you think about this, you will see that the more subjects that you do, the more of these tasks you will need to complete. So students who think they have lots of time are actually just deluded. When students come to my study skills clinic, this is the first thing I do with them. When students have coursework to do or huge tasks to complete, this is the technique I force them to use. I had one student who was complaining about an essay that counted toward their final grade that was due in two weeks. It was 1000 words long, so I suggested dividing it up at 200 words a day – very manageable. They had completed it within three days, exceeding their daily target. It turns out that the student had the wrong essay title but when they showed it to their supervisor a week early the supervisor spotted this and they were able to fix the problem. They could have really messed up if they didn't use this technique.

In his book *Man's Search for Meaning*, Victor Frankl wrote of his experiences of surviving the death camps during the Holocaust. He discusses the importance of working back from a goal and how it can help you. His experiences and ideas led to him developing a type of therapy that centred on goals and meaning in life. He is used by many self-help gurus as an example of the importance in the power of goals. Frankl is a great book to read if you want to see why goals are important.

Don't leave things to the last minute

Leaving important work to the last minute because you didn't take control is completely avoidable. It is terrible when people ask for extensions for deadlines close to the end. In most cases, these extensions are unnecessary because if they had planned it earlier they would have had a draft produced and feedback on how to improve the work. So much work is handed in that could be improved if the students had bothered planning it. I don't want to seem insensitive; If a person had a valid reason then that is fine, we just find that often they don't. If you genuinely cared about your studies then you wouldn't leave it to the last minute or to chance.

Be flexible

It is also useful to remember that you have to **be flexible**. Things happen which can affect study and create challenges to producing work on time. The quicker you adjust to the problems by writing your goals again, the greater control you can have. If you are pressed for time then you will have more work to do.

This habit of study goals is really useful. If you are someone who has difficulty doing this, then aim to have short-term goals that are manageable and work toward the bigger goals when you become successful at it.

Hofstadter's Law

Now is a good time to tell you about **Hofstadter's Law** by Douglas Hofstadter, a professor of cognitive science, which states that it always takes longer to do something than you expect, even when you take into account Hofstadter's Law. So it is a good idea to make sure that you give your goals enough time. Never finish them exactly on the deadline, try a few days before. This means you are not handing in a piece of work on the afternoon of the deadline with no opportunity to fix any mistakes, as is all too often the case for some students.

I work as an examiner for A levels in the UK; the techniques I described are central to me completing my tasks on time. The exam board understands the importance of deadlines and so sets a timeframe for when you have 25 per cent done, 66 per cent and then completion. So I divide it down by daily targets of what I need to achieve in order to have it completed. Using this technique, I am able to get ahead of my target by days. I can take control and work toward having time on the weekend with my family.

SUMMARY

1 Goals are central to taking control of your study. If you don't know what your goals are then seek advice from your teachers or instructors and look at course outlines. These things are really easy to do and could mean you get better grades.

2 Clear and precise goals are vital as they make your study more motivating and easier to complete.

3 The SMART technique is the best way to plan goals. Meaning all goals should be Specific, Measurable, Action-based, Realistic and Time-based.

4 The best way to set up goals is to work backwards from a deadline. So if you have a 2000-word essay to complete in ten days then you have 250 words to write a day and that will also give you time to prepare and revise your work. You can easily figure out what is expected of you on a daily basis and make changes

depending on time factors.

5 It is important to be flexible in the creation of goals. If you have missed a few days then you can adjust your deadlines and workload. You have five days to complete your 2000 word essay make it 500 words per day with time for revision if necessary.

6 Goal setting is the simple thing that motivates students to get started on their work and increase productivity. It breaks the bad habit of aimlessly sitting wondering what you're supposed to be doing.

4 Making good notes

If you find study really boring, then you are probably doing it wrong. I say this to my students and they pull faces or frown, they don't contemplate the idea that study could be engaging and interesting, even at times fun. The important thing is, study is supposed to be an *active process*.

Most students spend time reading the books passively and then just copying them out like some fifth century monk, or worse they highlight the text in yellow, blue and pink luminous ink that practically fills the books. If I said to you right now that you had to go get one of your textbooks, half read it and then write everything out but slightly shorter and then when you have done this colour in your notes yellow then spend the remaining time you have reading those notes over and over again, you would probably tell me to get lost, and you should as it is the least effective way to study.

You are not a fifth century monk so it is not necessary to just copy information out of a book and hope that somehow you will remember it all. The big error in all this is that you will start to recognise the books and notes and ideas but without knowing the ideas as well as you should for an exam. You would be better off **testing yourself after you have studied** to see what you have retained, therefore testing your strategy out.

In the exam you will be asked questions, you then have to try and collect the information out of your head and try to construct an answer in the exam. Given the time constraints and pressure, this is a challenge for most students and you may find that the essays that you have written for class produce better answers than those under timed conditions. The technique that I am going to mention now helps to overcome the problem of poor retention of information and poor study techniques. This can seem a bit boring to begin with, but stick with it as it produces more effective study.

Preview Question Read Review

To avoid taking a passive approach to study, people have suggested a technique called the **Preview Question Read Review** technique – **PQRR**. It comes in many formats but the one I have mentioned here is the easiest to use. I first learned about this technique in Aidan Moran's book *Managing Your learning at University.* It can triple the amount of information that you retain. Yes, that's right, it can *triple the amount of information you learn*, and will also help you create more useful notes.

Students can suffer from what I call the **error of recognition**, as I mentioned before. That is, they see the information on a page that they have read and assume that they know it. This is not the case, they merely *recognise* it. If a student in my class tells me 'we have already done this', I get them all to close their books and write the key points from memory and a different story emerges: they are unable to remember much of the information even though they feel they know it.

Before we begin the PQRR technique, read this:

The procedure is actually quite simple. First you arrange things into different groups. Of course, one pile may be sufficient depending on how much there is to do. If you have to go somewhere else due to lack of facilities that is the next step, otherwise you are pretty well set. It is important not to overdo things. That is, it is better to do too few things at once than too many. In the short run this may not seem important but complications can easily arise. A mistake can be expensive as well. At first the whole procedure will seem complicated.Soon, however, it will become just another facet of life. It is difficult to foresee any end to the necessity for this task in the immediate future, but then one never can tell, After the procedure is completed one arranges the materials into different groups again. Then they can be put into their appropriate places. Eventually they will be used once more and the whole cycle will then have to be repeated. However, that is part of life.

Now close the book and write that out on a piece of paper. Only kidding. Though if you do, try to see how much you recall and you will find that it is extremely difficult.

The paragraph you have just read was created by some memory researchers called Bransford and Johnson in 1972. When they presented participants with this in their study they found recall to be very poor. The paragraph makes little sense when you read it, it should make you think 'what are they going on about?' You may even need to reread it a few times. 'What procedure is quite simple?' you may ask yourself.

Bransford and Johnson divided their participants into two groups. The first group were just presented with the material and, as you can imagine, they had poor recall. The other group were told that the paragraph was about 'doing the laundry'. It made more sense. The second group had much better recall. Reading it now with that in mind it is easier to comprehend.

Doing the Laundry

The procedure is actually quite simple. First you arrange things into different groups. Of course, one pile may be sufficient depending on how much there is to do. If you have to go somewhere else due to lack of facilities that is the next step, otherwise you are pretty well set. It is important not to overdo

*things. That is, it is better to do too few
things at once than too many. In the short
run this may not seem important but
complications can easily arise. A mistake can
be expensive as well. At first the whole
procedure will seem complicated. Soon,
however, it will become just another facet of
life. It is difficult to foresee any end to the
necessity for this task in the immediate
future, but then one never can tell, After the
procedure is completed one arranges the
materials into different groups again. Then
they can be put into their appropriate
places. Eventually they will be used once
more and the whole cycle will then have to
be repeated. However, that is part of life.*

The problem most students have is that the way they approach study makes the information looks more like how you viewed the Bransford and Johnson paragraph. The information is just not retained. The technique I suggest helps to make it more like how the second group of participants saw the paragraph, which is more meaningful.

If you recognise that this is something that concerns you then you need to use the **Preview, Question, Read and Review technique**. I would suggest that you just try it and see if you can actually remember more.

The first thing to do is to get a chapter of a book or parts of a chapter and **Preview** it. This means you scan or survey the chapter you are going to read. You can check out the length and make a decision about how much is manageable in one sitting. Look at the charts, tables, the summary and the stupid cartoons they decided to put in as a futile attempt to add humour. This first stage gives you the opportunity to see what the chapter is about.

The next stage is to **Question**. This involves writing down key questions that you can turn into notes. During the preview stage you will find some chapter titles: so if the chapter title is *The difference between short-term and long-term memory,* your question would be 'What is the difference between short-term and long-term memory?'. My key advice is that you should have about **three main questions per study period**. For more labour intensive chapters it could be one question. This will make your reading less aimless and boring and the information far more meaningful. If you can't think of what questions to use then look at the course outline and/or past papers to help you come up with some questions.

According to Aidan Moran, 'successful students have questions in search for answers. Unsuccessful students have answers in search of questions.' Sometimes students just trust a book is full of the correct information but when they get to the exam they realise that it was wrong. If you are more question-focused, it will help you sift through the less useful material in your textbooks. Don't just rely on one book. If you want to learn you may need to have multiple books at your disposal; you may find another author is better at explaining the ideas.

The next stage is to **Read** in search of answers to your questions. You can **write down or bullet point your answers**. The answers are now your notes, they are labelled clearly and easier to find and study.

The final stage is the **Review** stage. This stage just checks that the information is in your head. You could take a break and then come back and **test yourself**. You could take a blank piece of paper and test to see how you could answer the questions. If you can't remember some of the information then you can go back over it.

I wouldn't dream of studying without using this technique. There are some longer versions of this approach. Burns and Sinfield suggest the **QOOQRRR** (Cooker) technique: **Question, Overview, Overview, Question, Read, Re-read and Review**. That is a little excessive though. Payne and Whittaker use an approach to the one I suggest called the **SQ3R**: **Survey, Question, Read, Recite and Review**. People sometimes like the recite bit before testing themselves.

Whichever technique, this approach works so much better than passive approaches to reading textbooks. While it does take a little time to form a habit of using it, the results are much better than not using it. As you are going through the stages, you might want to take a break before you test yourself. It is vital though that you actually come back and test yourself. You can then check to see if you have actually retained the information.

 If your breaks are longer than your study period then you are doing it wrong. So coming back to a quick test that you have designed can help trigger a more active study period.

Shorthand

When taking notes, you should consider using and or creating shorthand symbols. This speeds up the process of note taking and you can make them work for you. You'll be the only person reading them (unless you're sharing notes and studying with a friend) so they can be anything that you want, but here are some existing examples:

> *bf = before*
>
> *i.e. = that is*
>
> *e.g. = for example*
>
> *w/ = with*

∴ = therefore

> = bigger than

Try inventing your own. Remember, this is all about speeding up your note making processes so whatever works for you, go for it. You could draw pictures in your notes to bring them to life. See **Chapter 5 Creative study activities** below for more ideas.

Mnemonics

Linked to the point above, it can be useful to employ mnemonic devices to help have shortcuts to remembering meaningful chunks of information. When we talk about mnemonics, we mean systems or strategies which aid memory. They can be based on visual or verbal aids. There are many different types of these so called verbal mnemonics, the most common of which are acronyms and acrostics. They can be really helpful when you have to learn subject material for exams that otherwise you might not be interested in. You can make them as personal, funny or rude as you like. After all, nobody is going to use them except for you, unless you want to share them. If you have to learn something that has key parts or sequences, then this is a great tool.

Acronyms are a verbal mnemonic that construct a word from the first letter of each word. When I teach students how to evaluate in their essays we can use the Acronyms SEE (Statement, Explain, Example) or SEX (A bit of a cheat but students remember it more – Statement, Explain, eXample) or PEE (Point, Explain, Example).

Another more useful technique is an **acrostic**. This is where you create a new sentence based on the first letter of the information you need to remember. For instance, if I wanted to remember the main subdivisions of the embryonic vertebrate brain: pro-encephalon or forebrain, the mesencephalon or midbrain and the rhombencephalon or hindbrain, I could take the letters PFMMRH and create the sentence Pete Found My Mum's Red Hat. That's a bit bland, I know. You'll probably find that if you make them funny or rude they will become more memorable.

Some other examples of acrostics can be Blood's functions: Old Charlie Foster Hates Women Having Dull Clothes. It stands for oxygen (transport), carbon dioxide (transport), food, heat, waste, hormones, disease, clotting. Or you could have I Pee More After Tea Constantly to remember the lifecycle of cells (Interphase, Prophase, Metaphase, Anaphase, Telophase, Cytokinesis).

My English Professor in Dublin created what he suggested is a great way to bluff your way through the analysis of a poem. He suggested using FSLITST or the F SLITS T. He said if you wanted to talk about the poem, you could think of the Form, Style, Language, Imagery, Tone, Symbolism and Theme.

The benefit of using these techniques is that it allows you to spend some time thinking about what it is you have to learn. You can have a bit of fun with it and the methods can be used for a variety of subjects. You can even use these to help you to spell words. My favourite is DIARRHOEA: Dashing In A Rush, Running Harder Or Else Accident! or Dining In A Rough Restaurant: Hurry, Otherwise Expect Accidents! and finally Diarrhoea Is A Really Runny Heap Of Endless Amounts.

SUMMARY

1 It is important that you do not rely on passive approaches to study. They are dangerous as they give the illusion that you know something when in fact you don't. Reading your notes or just writing them out with no clear focus are examples of passive approaches to study and not great techniques to employ.

2 Study needs to be active. Use the Preview Question Read Review Technique as it helps you to process your notes in a much more meaningful way.

3 It is vital during your study that you test yourself to see how much you know. If you don't remember

anything then read your notes again. It is much better to realise early on that the previous two hours of study have not been effective, rather than realising it in the exam, where you can do nothing.

4 A proven technique to help you remember information is to employ mnemonics like acrostics and acronyms.

5 Creative study activities

Creativity is just connecting things. When you ask creative people how they did something, they feel a little guilty because they didn't really do it, they just saw something. It seemed obvious to them after a while. That's because they were able to connect experiences they've had and synthesize new things.

Steve Jobs

By now you should have a clearer idea of how to become more active in the way you study. Even if you just use the PQRR technique that I have suggested, then you are moving away from a passive approach towards more active study. One of the best parts of this technique is the one most students don't consider that important: the review stage. Testing yourself in the comfort of your own home is a very good way of seeing what you know.

I am going to make a few suggestions in this chapter that are a little more creative. They serve as extra activities to do and they reduce the boredom that comes from passive study. Many of them rely upon using phones or tablets constructively. With the advancement of technology you can find better ways of using your smartphones or tablets to help you to study. I will mention some useful methods in this chapter.

Many people have such sophisticated technology at their disposal and yet they use it for the most basic of functions. People own expensive macs that they only use for emails, Facebook or YouTube. I have seen students become experts at stupid games that, while they are acceptable for short term entertainment, severely limit their time and ability to study properly.

Once a student complained about not really learning and how he was worried about the exams. I asked him to write down how he had learned the things he knew and make a list of these techniques. It was surprising that so many of the techniques he listed belonged to creative techniques I had forced him to use. I told him to use those techniques more. It's that simple.

Most of this is not rocket science. It is testing to see what works and doing more of that and less of what doesn't.

This chapter is about trying out those different techniques to help you see what would work for you, but you *must* test it and see what makes a difference. So while I list a bunch of alternative ways to study here, the simple suggestion is that you make a list of the ones that seem appealing to you and then test their effectiveness. Don't test too early, as you will want to give them a chance to work. I have tested all of these on my students and found that they greatly improve their understanding and their grades.

I started looking at creative ways to study when I read about the importance of being creative in two study skills books. When I scanned the books to find some of the creative techniques they had just mentioned, mind maps and recording yourself, I thought I could do better than that and so began my journey into creative study. I thought I would be able to steal some ideas from my students, so I began asking my students about what ideas they had for making their study more interesting and creative.

The results were depressing, although I did have a limited sample. Most mentioned just mind maps or recording themselves, just like the books. I asked my students if they liked mind maps and they mostly said no. This is the horrifying part; every one of the students asked had to attend a class teaching them how to do it. Tony Buzan, the guy who claimed to have invented mind maps, has made a fortune out of this idea. Yes, they do work but only if you use them, and some students don't like them. Over the years I have asked people attending my lectures on study skills if they use them and only a small amount put up their hands. It's criminal how many study skills seminars have been centered on the idea. So for years I have thought about lots of creative techniques to get students to study.

Here are a select few I have found, created or, just as Steve Jobs said, connected. Try some out and see if they help you. You can use these for times when you're sitting in front of the TV or at home for the holidays. They make great revision tools and start you working when you feel like you don't want to do anything.

The one thing I would suggest about the creative techniques is that you test them. That is exactly what psychologists do when they are experimenting with new techniques, interventions or therapies. They may create an experiment that looks at normal approaches to study or a control and compare it to the technique they are testing. You, as a student, are in a perfect position to do this. In your spare time, try something I suggest and test to see if it works. I would suggest that you try the ideas a couple of times and then evaluate whether they work for you. I ask all my students if they find study boring. For those that do, I tell them that they are doing it wrong.

Turn your notes into presentations

Many students find their own notes quite boring to read. It is important that you find a way to make them more engaging. One simple and really quite creative way is to **turn your notes into a PowerPoint or Keynote presentation**. It doesn't matter what package you use, both Apple and Microsoft Office have made theirs into apps to use on your smartphone or tablet (and of course, others are available). The great thing is, you can make them look good. Most students, when given the task to make a presentation, will put everything on it and then read it out word for word. While this is extremely boring to watch (though I completely understand why students do it), it does make for good notes. You can use them on your phone. You don't even have to type everything. You could take photos of parts of your books or embed someone else's slides. This task is excellent for complicated material. You can even export them as movies.

One thing I suggest to my students is that they **create PowerPoint flashcards**. Write a question in the title of the slide and animate the answer to appear. It is a really simple but really effective way of testing yourself. If you have taken the photos, you can use shapes to obscure or hide the main points and then you can guess the things as you go along, creating a perfect revision tool.

Animate your notes

I mentioned earlier that you can record your notes which is so easy with today's technology. In fact, if you add audio to the PowerPoint, you have created a movie. Though it will be far from a blockbuster, it is something that you can use as a more engaging interaction with your notes. Why not make an animation of your notes? You can do this by using some apps on the iPad and could add audio or edit them using iMovie or other movie-making apps. You can actually do this in many ways using a phone, tablet or laptop. You can use stop motion apps and take pictures of the notes as you wish them to appear. You can also use apps that do the work for you and draw pictures, or even have your notes slowly appear. Some really great apps for animation include; iStopMotion, Stop Motion, Animation HD, AnimationDesk, Motion and PicPac.

You can draw your notes on any of the note making apps and take screenshots, and this can be edited together to create simple notes that you can watch.

I once had a student who complained about being too tired to do any work, so I gave her and the other students the task of creating an animation. I chose the most boring topic I could. I started them off and then left them to it. They all had a free lesson after so when I asked them if they wanted to stop or finish the task they all opted to finish and stayed about 45 minutes longer than the lesson. This is when I realised how powerful some of these techniques can be, especially for subjects or topics you're less interested in. You could use a whiteboard to create the canvas. Set up your camera and aim it at the whiteboard and just take photos every few words; the results can be better than simple passive approaches to study.

Turn your notes into posters

A really simple idea to make creative notes is to turn them into posters or graphics. You can do it by hand to create nice artistic posters to put on the wall. Posters are great ways to put important exam tips, essay writing tips or step by step guides in view. If you don't want to hang them up you can always just keep these graphics in your notes.

Infographics stands for *information graphics*, which present difficult information in a visually pleasing way. It is suggested that they help people to take in complex ideas and make connections in a quicker way. When you see infographics they are so much more visually appealing than reading lists of figures or tables in a book or during a presentation. I have found that when I present with lists of numbers students will remember some of them but will become confused or bored quite quickly. If you are studying something that has lots of data that you need to learn then it is probably a good idea to create infographics. You can create your own infographics online with lots of different infographic websites. One website called visual.ly allows you to view other people's infographics and make stunning notes. Another website called infogr.am also allows you to create infographics online to use. You could also try easel.ly.

Why write it all out anyway?

Some students tell me that it helps them to remember it. However, I have already mentioned how students have a tendency to take a passive approach to study and this sometimes involves just writing out their notes exactly as they are in the book. Maybe they will shorten the notes. They may even rehearse the information over and over again. A major problem with this is that they have not placed much meaning into the work, it therefore may not have the depth that they need when it comes to exams.

There is also the problem that people have a tendency to daydream or lose concentration when they are just taking notes and writing them out, word for word. What I suggest here is simple, you can **create useful notes that can be more colourful and nice to look at**. If you have more than one text book for a subject that you are studying then you can really take advantage of this idea: find a key question or essay or something that you need to learn. Then get an A3 sheet of paper and write out the question on the side or in the middle. Then search your textbooks for information needed to answer the question. Read the information that is important and when you have found every important detail that you need in as many books as you can, scan or photocopy the sections you need. I have found that if you reduce the size by about 70%

you can fit more on the A3 sheet. It does look nice if you can photocopy or print out in colour. I would then cut out all the useful information and then stick it on the sheet. This is so helpful to get you to select the correct information and creates really useful revision tools.

I have mentioned the importance of testing yourself so here are some linked ideas that allow you to test yourself, but in a more creative way.

Flashcards

The point of flashcards is not to write everything you know down on them; that would be just a version of mini notes, which many students don't find that effective. **The real idea is that you have a question on one side and the answer on the other**. Then during a study session you can flash the cards and guess the answer.

Flashcards were classically used for language but used in the right way they can be very useful for the study of any subject. Some students really believe that writing lots and lots of information really helps with the making of flash cards. The only problem with this is that it can create another attempt at passive study. The key is to learn what is on the cards and to test yourself often. You can be creative in how you make the cards. If you made a presentation or notes then you can print them out and put them on the cards. You can print the presentations that you made on Keynote or PowerPoint as handouts, you can then print out lots of slides per page. Cut these up and place them on the flash cards, then write a question on the other side.

There is also a really simple idea that I mentioned before in the section on cutting and pasting notes. In a similar fashion you can take text books and scan them or photocopy them, if you shrink them down to about 50–70 per cent the size of the text book then you can cut out key terms or tables that are in the text book and use these as the answers to the questions. This saves lots of time when it comes to the making of flashcards. It is also something that you can do when you are tired. You could even create a factory line at home. Print out what you want and get your family involved. Convince them to do it. At the beginning rush through them, making more than anyone else, then when they finally speed up to try and overtake you, you can slow down. You can sit back and let your family create some of the best revision cards you need.

Keynote/PowerPoint flashcards

If you made presentations using PowerPoint or Keynote in the previous chapter then you can easily turn these into **interactive flashcards**. The process is really simple. When you create a presentation, you will need to put a question in the title part of the slide at the top, then you answer the question in the main body of the slide. Using animations, you can slowly build the answer with each press of the spacebar and test yourself as you are going along. This is where you can save time if you have already built lots of presentations; you can cut and paste the slides onto a new presentation. You can take photos of the notes that you want to learn or the diagrams that you need to know. If you have created a diagram or taken a picture of one you need to learn, you can then then place shapes over the information so they are hidden and then make them disappear when you you hit the spacebar on the computer or a simple swipe gesture on the iPad so you can guess all the major parts that you need to know, and instantly see if you are correct. Taking photos of the textbooks and hiding them with shapes or blurring them is a really creative way of doing this.

Post-it note quiz

A simple idea is **using Post-It notes to test your knowledge**. Post-It notes are ideal for this as you can stick them all over your computer screen or desk and when you come back from a break you can begin to test what you remember. The idea is simple – write a question on the front of the Post-it note and then, on the reverse (the sticky side), write your answer. The size of the Post-It notes will force you to keep your questions and answers brief. I have discussed the idea of getting back to work with students after they take a short break. Many students have no problem continuing with work, it is just the feeling they have after they take a break, some just don't want to return to their desk or get distracted by other things. This idea could help prevent that. They can quickly create a few Post-It notes that cover what they have been studying and then stick them on the desk, or on their computer screen. They can then come back and test to see if they understand and know what they have been studying.

As you make more and more of these Post-It notes, you can **randomly choose questions to test**. Then divide them into piles: the ones you got correct and the ones you did not get correct. You could place them on the stairs leading up to your room, so you can test to see how you are doing before you even reach your desk.

Cut and sort

Another thing that I find with students is that they can remember some topics teachers have taught them but forget how. When I ask them, this technique pops up. This idea is a really simple way to create a quick way of testing yourself. Lots of teachers hand out cut-up diagrams or tables that the students have to put back together in the right order. You'll find that most text books are filled with different types of graphics that are supposed to help you understand the material. What I have found is students will take a moment and look at these graphics or tables and not really process the information. They could be flowcharts, or tables describing the differences/similarities or strengths and weaknesses of important things.

All you have to do is **photocopy or scan the material. Then cut it up**. If you are photocopying or scanning a book you don't own, it would be a good idea to have a couple of copies of whatever you are cutting up so you can check back to see if you have it correct; one to keep as reference and the other to cut up. You can even do this with the main text in a book. Cut out the sections and cut off the titles if you can find the right headings that go with the sections then you understand the material. You can easily make your own tables or step-by-step explanations of a theory or biological process, you could even create timelines of historical or economic events. It is a really quick way to test to see if you know the stages involved in some processes.

 I have created some **homemade pin boards** by sticking together some cardboard into a square and covering it with paper. The students can then pin the correct things in the right order.

One alternative use for this is to **cut up an essay and see if you can put it back together**. I have seen this used as a way of checking if the essay and all the parts belong together.

Unlucky dip

I have found that some students are overwhelmed by the amount of questions that they have to do. They will spend a huge part of the revision period trying to decide what questions to tackle. A creative approach to this is to make a document with lots of the questions typed out, or just a photocopy of the past exam papers, once the relevant topic has been covered. Then, **cut them the questions and roll them into balls, find a box, envelope or hat and put them all in**. As you go through your study you can keep adding to the pile of questions. Therefore you know that you have studied all the content for the questions in the hat. Exams tend to be a random collection of questions so this method prepares you for the coming exams.

The beauty of this idea is that if you have to do lots of questions in an exam with some long questions and some short questions then this task could mean that for some revision sessions you may only get short questions. Put by a set amount of time that you will test yourself on; 30 minutes would be a good starting point. Then, **pull out some random questions one**

by one and do them. You could have a box/hat/envelope for each subject or each unit. This forces you to do questions that you may want to avoid when you are studying.

Blank piece of paper

Nothing really creative about a blank piece of paper, but when it comes to testing how much you can remember about a topic, this might be all that you need. I start many lessons by saying to my students, 'on a blank piece of paper...' and then ask them some set questions. It is a useful way to start or end a study session too. It is useful if you create essay plans and time how quickly you can plan the key points in an essay or create a 'bare bones' or scaffolded answer, which is slightly more information but not the whole essay.

Spider diagram

It is important that you do write essays, but if this is only what you are doing then it could be what is slowing you down. If you have three topics that are essay based then that is a lot of writing. No wonder some people find it boring. I suggest to my students that they **regularly create spider diagrams of the answers**. Spider diagrams are simply a circle with lines coming out; resembling a spider.

Teach someone

Create some aids to help someone else learn.
Working in a group is great if you are really social. You have to work though; it is not a good idea to meet up without a clear plan. This technique really helps you to get to grips with complex ideas. If you can explain them and help someone else understand then you will be better at answering questions. Any teacher will tell you, the tricky questions asked by students in class really improve a teacher's own knowledge. Standing at the front of a class teaching study skills and being asked questions by students has helped me out and given me a better understanding of the subject.

Study in a group

This only works if study is more of the focus than the social element of this. Students have a tendency to get distracted easily. Some students are very sociable and do not enjoy the idea of spending hours alone in a room. To them it feels like a punishment. This is why it may be worth combining the study with more social practices. You must only consider this idea if you can actually work with the people you are planning to meet with.

When I was in university I studied advanced statistics with a group of people, because we did not want to study this on our own. It was a complicated topic, but the social element of studying together made it more fun, which helped us learn more. I began to love statistics and still do. I have to teach concepts that I once thought were boring and complicated.

It is worth looking at some of your friends and seeing if they would be interested in studying with you. It may be fun at times and you *will* distract each other. However, if you find that you are *only* distracting each other then you would be best to stop this and just see each other when you are not studying.

Coffee shops are a great place to meet and go over the topics together and maybe you could use some of the previous techniques to study. If you test each other using some of the ideas, then all you need is a tablet and a half an hour or an hour regularly to help improve your grades. If you find a friend who is passionate about a subject that you are not, it may be worth talking to them about this subject and learning from them. If you have created flash cards or PowerPoints then you could use these as the basis of the study. If you are not really all that motivated then you could take the time to make an animation together or a quick movie. This would be time better spent than just sitting and doing nothing.

I have found that if you spend a little time each week building creative projects then, in a short while, you would have lots of useful resources when it comes to revising together. You could share your notes and see how you could divide up the tasks. I have encouraged some of my students to work together in the past and they have benefited massively when it comes to the exams. I have not cared if they like each other or if they normally 'hang out', I just give them a task or selection of tasks to do and I have found that they will produce more work if they have someone to work with. If you make some of the more time consuming projects with someone else then you may be able to make things while you are just sitting around chatting.

Organise and sort your notes

This is far more creative than sitting around and doing nothing in the evening. Students find it hard to get started on their work for many reasons. So, if you can't think of what to do, you should organise your notes. See that they are all up to date or that you have completed them.

One simple way to check your notes is something I call **auditing your notes**. All you have to do is get a past exam paper or questions that have been asked on the course you are sitting and see if you can answer it using your notes. If you can't then you need to add more information to your notes. This is far better than the alternative; learning the notes off by heart only to realise during the exam that you hadn't covered something adequately, because by then, it's too late. I constantly see students wanting to use books to answer questions and while this is a great way of acquiring information, you would be better trying to answer the question using only your notes and head.

Download the subject syllabus and **create a syllabus checklist**: Go through your notes to see that every aspect of the syllabus is covered and in the right level of detail.

Do your notes have **headings or titles**? Sometimes students have written notes by just copying out of the book, paying very little attention to what they are writing. Read through your notes, check to see what they are saying and add headings at the top.

If you are in the habit of writing notes but not organising them or just shoving them into your bag then it is a good idea to sit down and find them and **put the notes in order**. In terms of study it will help you out if you do this as often as possible. You may find that, as the course progresses and you learn more material, the notes need reordering. This is a great chance to go over what you know and how different concepts are connected to each other. This practice will help you out when it gets closer to exams.

Another important part of checking your notes is that you **find out if everything you've written is useful or important**. Sometimes at the very beginning of a course students have been given basic materials that are no longer relevant. You may need to separate these and only have the really important information in your files.

If you don't take notes in class then you have to work twice as hard when you get home, making up these missing notes. I make a habit of checking my students' notes in class and they appreciate it. It is amazing to see how much random information people have in their notes. It could be down to simple things like the passive approach to note making, getting tired or stopping but not coming back and finishing that part of their notes. So, checking them is vital if you are going to learn them and attempt to use them in the exam.

A game of Liar

I like this simple idea, it involves a group of people studying the same topic. You nominate someone to discuss an essay or answer a question. Then the others have to listen to the detail and accuracy. As soon as someone starts to stumble, lose focus or become inaccurate then you shout 'Liar!'. I would suggest that you add a timer and see who can go the longest without having someone in the group calling out. However, if you do shout 'Liar!' and you can't explain why then some sort of penalty needs to be dispensed. This game could be played in a café or at lunch, but *not* in a library. The game helps you create a depth and clarity to your answers. You can buy buzzers if you want, or download them on your phone. That adds an element of seriousness to the game, which can help some people focus.

Make a list of feedback

One thing I have noticed with students is that sometimes they will ignore the feedback you have given them. The feedback may be written in red writing on the top of a page or as little comments throughout your paper. Far too often students concentrate on the grade. They will ask 'what do I need to do?' After a while they will not remember what you have said to them. So it is really important that you gather together all the exams, essays and homework and start **making a list of the comments**. If you have a teacher who has ticked the exam questions but not said much then you could go back to them and ask for more detailed feedback or tips on how to improve your work. Teachers are in the habit of repeating themselves so just ask them again if you are unsure.

I have had students during study skills telling me that the teacher does not tell them what to do. I had them bring me in some exam papers. The reality was that the teacher had written all over the paper, 'Read the questions', 'Make sure you plan your answers' and 'elaborate your points'; these tips are clear. The feedback might seem brief, but there's nothing wrong with succinct feedback as a starting point. In fact, too much detailed feedback can reduce the ability of a student to think for themselves.

It is common for people to forget what tips they have been given but it is essential that you look for this feedback and then go about correcting it. Some of my top students have constantly asked about what they need to do to improve and will produce more work than I can comfortably mark. They also crave feedback, and this is what helps with study.

Use file dividers to store the valuable feedback given to you by your teachers. Keep a note of important exam tips given by the teachers on how to improve your grades and make an attempt at overcoming these difficulties. A really simple checklist to create is to **have a table that has the problems you need to address with your work and tips on how to improve**. You could add checklists to see that you have attempted to overcome these when you attempt your work in the future.

Use your smartphone

If you are using your smartphone then learn to use it properly. It is one of the best pieces of technology to land in your hands in the last few years. Think of ways of being creative with your smartphone during your study. **Use the timer** to do questions that mimic exam timing. **Take photos of parts of the books to add to PowerPoints** rather than writing the whole thing out, or **take screenshots of pdfs** to use in the same way. You can create powerful animations of your notes and watch them, as mentioned above. There are many apps that can be used for study that can really change the way you learn, you can quickly become creative and turn your smartphone or tablet into a really useful tool for study. I will have mentioned some apps earlier in this book, but I won't go into great detail as apps change in popularity. Look for apps and think of ways you could use them to make study more portable and creative. The limits to how creative and active you make your study is up to you. While you may think some of these ideas aren't that great, I have found really positive results when I encourage students to use them. The important thing is that if you are finding something difficult then you may have to do something creative and time consuming so you can add depth to your learning.

SUMMARY

1 Find ways of studying that interest you.

2 Try alternative ways to study.

3 Test to see if they work for you.

4 Use your technology for actual study and not just social media.

6 Dealing with stress

Below are some simple approaches to handling study-related stress but I need to emphasise that having a master's in Psychology doesn't make me an expert in dealing with stress. I'm not and neither are you or your friends. Be sensible and see a doctor if stress is getting the better of you or if you think you might be showing signs of depression.

Stress is something that students have to deal with on a regular basis. Having no stress at all (in relation to study) is quite rare. There are many things that can lead to stress. It could be that you have a high level of demand or workload or that you have little (or feel that you have little) control over that demand. It could be that you have poor coping strategies when studying towards your exams. If you find yourself procrastinating more than usual, this could be a sign that you are experiencing stress.

I have mentioned the importance of having goals. This can give you back the control you need to get tasks done. Putting tasks off may be due to the fact that you feel that the tasks are too overpowering. One definition of stress that I find really useful describes stress as:

'the discrepancy a person someone has between the perceived demands of the environment and their perceived ability to cope with those demands.'

The important part is the word *perceived*; people will tell themselves that the task is too big, or they are too weak or they will simply say 'I can't do this'.

What is happening biologically

I will explain some powerful techniques to deal with irrational perceptions that people have in relation to stress. But first, what is actually happening to your body when you feel stressed? What is happening *biologically* is important. We have evolved to deal with stress of a very different nature to the causes of stress today. The purpose was to aid our survival, a time when you were more likely to be caught by a bear in the woods than have to do an exam. Once we perceive something as stressful, we have two pathways that become activated in the body's response to stress, each with a purpose of helping us survive. Brace yourself, here comes some science.

The *hypothalamus*, at the base of the brain, is alerted by the potentially stressful situation, such as the sudden appearance of a bear. The two pathways activated by the hypothalamus are the *pituitary-adrenal system* and the *sympathomedullary pathway*. For the pituitary-adrenal system, the pituitary gland that resides in the brain and is connected to the hypothalamus is known as the *master gland*, releasing a number of hormones into the bloodstream. So this stressful encounter triggers the hypothalamus to release a stress hormone from the pituitary gland called *adrenocorticotrophic hormone* (ACTH). This hormone then travels to the *adrenal cortex*, part of the adrenal gland which is located on the kidneys. This stimulates the release of *corticosteriods* such as *cortisol* and *corticosterone*. This all happens to inhibit your immune system and your tissue inflammation. It also releases energy from the liver, mobilising these stored energy reserves, providing us with glucose and fatty acids that can be burned up in physical activity. The activation of the sympathomedullary pathway is signalled by the hypothalamus through nervous impulses travelling rapidly from the brainstem to the *adrenal medulla*, also on the kidneys. It causes the release of *adrenaline* and *noradrenaline* into the bloodstream, which in turn causes an increase in heart rate and blood pressure, speeding up the supply of oxygen to the muscles so it can be used in physical activity.

The function of these pathways is to help protect us in stressful situations and help us with our fight or flight reactions. So, back to the bear, this system will help us fight (bad idea), or we can run (better idea). When and if we get away we can calm down and reassess the situation. This all sounds reasonable with a bear, but not so useful when we are dealing with an exam or workload.

If we have extended periods of stress as a result of

changing workloads and the demands of study and life then it can result in suppression of the immune system, useful as a short-term stress response, but horrible for extended periods like the exams season. It can cause illness, at the worst possible time: when we are doing our exams.

I think it's important that you understand the biological processes which produce the feeling of stress, as this can help you recognise these processes in yourself and ride them out while you work on strategies to reduce stress.

Factors that cause stress

So back to the things that causes students stress. According to Andrew Northedge, factors that lower morale and cause stress are varied and include **disruption to your daily life**; so much study to fit in, which can create pressures on social commitments and leisure interests. **Information overload** can also be a problem, including too much to take in: timetables, tasks, deadlines, and personal pressures you may face. A **loss of confidence** in your own abilities, apparent lack of progress, and doubts that you will make it to the end of the course. **Lack of structure** in your life. Feeling disorganised and not in control of events. **Dislocation**, maybe feeling that your studies are distancing you from your family, friends and community. They could also include everyday crises like **feeling overwhelmed** by the work, too many challenging and complicated tasks and little idea where to start. **Not being able to get started**, struggling to achieve a plan, **feeling that you will never finish, hating what you've written, feeling inarticulate**. Things that could be described as **'a bad day at the office'**: You leave your notes on the bus, the library is closed when you get there, your internet connection breaks down, your printer runs out of ink.

Disagreeable course elements: A tiresome book, not finding the books that you need, an irritating teacher. Disappointing results, a presentation goes badly, an assignment grade is worse than you expected, your teacher seems only to find fault.

Obsession with grades, an irrational concern over why you lost five marks on your last essay, or why your tutor made that criticism, when actually you are doing just fine. **Exam anxiety**: the exam looms like a distant black cloud casting a shadow over your enjoyment of the course.

These are a list of different pressures and stresses that Northedge suggests can be disastrous for students. If this list makes you feel a little stressed just reading it then pay attention to the tasks that follow and actually attempt to deal with your stress. Remember the goals I discussed earlier? It can truly eliminate the problems of organising, procrastinating, feeling like you will never finish and the feeling of lack of progress to name but a few of the stress factors mentioned above.

Cognitive Behavioural Therapy (CBT)

Dealing with stress is an important skill to learn if you want to achieve the best results in the exams. You don't have to be a genius to figure that out, yet so many students do nothing when it comes to dealing with stress. Most of the techniques that a person uses for dealing with stress are anything but supportive and can be downright dangerous.

Avoiding work or **procrastination** is one option that students use and this makes them more stressed, creating a vicious cycle of avoiding work and then getting even more stressed. There can be **a tendency to be emotional** about study – we've all called up our best friend and moaned about the essay deadline on Tuesday – when in fact you should be more practical in your approach. If you had a breakup then emotionally dealing with it is useful, but not so much use when you have essays due, or exams looming.

 The approach that is very useful in terms of moving past an emotional way of coping into a more practical look or rational approach is **Cognitive Behavioural Therapy** (CBT). It is a therapy that is used primarily to treat anxiety and depression though it is successful with other psychological problems too.

CBT was developed by two psychologists, Albert Ellis and Aaron Beck, in the 1960s. Earlier in the chapter, we defined stress as '*the discrepancy between the perceived demands of the environment and your perceived ability to cope with those demands'.* You may see why CBT will help because if your perceptions are negative or distorted then it will be difficult to cope with the demands of study.

The main goal of CBT is to alter the errors or maladaptive thinking people have and as a result alter the behaviour that comes in response. Research has shown that CBT is really effective in dealing with exam anxiety. There are some errors in thinking that are quite common, these errors are sometimes referred to as *cognitive distortions* and make us believe things that are not true. In fact, Beck believed that they cause us to have negative thoughts about ourselves, the world and our future. This can be detrimental when it comes to study. Getting rid of some of these errors in thinking about yourself, study, exams and your ability to succeed is a way of reducing your stress and improving productivity.

I have listed some of the common errors in thinking and related them to examples with study. These are, however, distortions and they can cause you to fall into habitual ways of thinking which can cause you to behave in ways that are not supportive of study. Once you have found which ones you use, you are beginning to tackle your anxiety and stress. Don't despair if you notice that you are prone to some or most of these types of thinking. I have included how to use this approach to target or test your thoughts after a selection of these cognitive distortions or errors in thinking.

Filtering

We take the negative details and magnify them while filtering out all positive aspects of a situation. So, in terms of study, you may get a bad grade in a subject and think you are no good at that subject and then you will remember or think about the mistakes you have made. Some students search the paper and ignore the questions that they got full marks on, instead they zoom in on the weaker responses and feel bad.

I was dealing with a student once who kept talking about his problems with exams and how he failed in them. When I asked him his grades he said he got two As and one D. He was so focused on the D that he ignored the good grades and told himself that he was no good at studying. If anything he was two thirds 'good' at study.

If your teacher is giving you feedback about why the grades are low then look at that feedback and make changes.

Filtering sometimes means that a person will discount or minimise the positives. Rejecting good things as if they don't matter. If they did well in an exam, it was just down to luck or it was an easy exam or they tell themselves that most people would do well. If you give them positive feedback, they think you are just being nice. This means it is difficult for them to appreciate the times they have succeeded. This type of filtering reduces motivation and can make it difficult to appreciate what you need to do to improve.

Polarised Thinking (or 'Black and White' Thinking)

We have to be perfect or we're a failure – there is no middle ground according to this cognitive distortion. You place people or situations in *either/or* categories, with no shades of grey or allowing for the complexity of most people and situations. If your performance falls short of perfect, you see yourself as a total failure. This can be detrimental to your study. People will ignore the feedback that they have been given. After all, the purpose of study is to learn, so if you are making mistakes rather than thinking you can't do something, you could look at how can you fix these problems. This can lead students to believe that if they can't solve this problem, learn the material or remember the information, then they must give up altogether. The problem with this type of thinking is that you end up just deciding that study is too difficult and not worth it.

Over-generalisation

With this particular bias, we come to a general conclusion based on a single incident or a single piece of evidence. If something bad happens only once, we expect it to happen over and over again. A person may see a single, unpleasant event as part of a never-ending pattern of defeat. This is best seen when people say, 'I will always fail' or 'I never pass exams' based on the fact that one or two of their exams went bad. People will rewrite their past to fit these over-generalisations, rather than looking to see how true the belief is. Over-generalising based on a single case is not correct: statistically or logically.

Catastrophising

We expect disaster to strike, no matter what. In *CBT for Dummies* this was referred to as 'turning molehills into mountains'. For example, if I do poorly on one question, I am going to fail the exams. The reality is that exams rarely hinge on one question alone. You may feel that if you make a single mistake then you will never get to university, never get a job and so on. You will feel like the one mistake means you have messed up everything. I tend to seek out my students after an exam to see how they are doing. I once had a student who had panicked during the first exam and froze. She didn't finish the exam but felt that she was going to fail again and never go to uni. I calmed her down, reminded her that she had three more papers to do. She had, when it came to results, done poorly in the exam, but as we were able to work on keeping calm for the rest of the exam period, she performed better in the other three, got a good result and has finished university since.

Fortune telling

Believing that you can predict the future, and then believing that this future will happen. We are all (to a certain degree) guilty of this. Sometimes we are right, but often we are not. This tends to fit in with catastrophising; thinking that we are going to fail the exams, or that we are going to mess up no matter what we do. It is very difficult to motivate yourself if you think like this.

Personalisation

Personalisation is a distortion where a person believes that everything others do or say is some kind of direct, personal reaction to themselves. We also compare ourselves to others, trying to determine who is smarter, better looking, etc. This bias can lead people to feel that the teacher or instructor doesn't like them or thinks they are stupid. If, during a study skills session,

I see a student who looks distracted, were I to personalise it, then I would feel that I am boring them or they don't like my instruction or they don't like me. The truth is it *might* be that or it might be many other reasons as to why they look bored. You can't get through to everyone, people may dislike you for rational or irrational reasons. The key is that it doesn't stop you from realising that it is not all about you.

Should and *mustabatory* thinking

We have a list of ironclad rules about how others and about how we should behave. People who break the rules make us angry, and we feel guilty when we violate these rules. A person may often believe they are trying to motivate themselves with shoulds and shouldn'ts, as if they have to be punished before they can do anything. Ellis said, 'don't should all over yourself'. The problem is that these pressurising words, instead of motivating us, add more pressure. Motivation disappears and feelings of guilt kick in. There are many of these pressurising words: *Must*, *Have to*, *Ought to*. There are also extremist words to look out for like *Always* and *Never*, they are very rarely true. 'I always forget to do things', 'I never finish my work'. They also create pressure on you and make you want to avoid doing study or work. Ellis also coined the term *mustabatory thinking*, which is thinking certain ideas and assumptions must be true for you to be happy. When you say things like 'I must do well in tests' or 'I am worthless', then these thoughts, while creating pressure, can also lead to low moods and stress.

Emotional Reasoning

We believe that what we feel must be true without evaluating or reasoning. If we feel stupid and boring, then we must be stupid and boring. You assume that your unhealthy emotions reflect the way things really are – 'I feel it, therefore it must be true'. Mistaking feelings for facts means that you have to work harder to check the reality of the feelings. You may feel down, sad and upset when in fact you are tired because you have been working all day. The term *Hangry* describes the feeling of being angry because you are hungry.

Labelling

We generalise one or two qualities into a negative global judgment. These are extreme forms of generalising, and are also referred to as 'labelling' and 'mislabelling'. Instead of describing an error in the context of a specific situation, a person will attach an unhealthy label to themselves.

For example, they may say, 'I'm a loser' in a situation where they failed at a specific task. Or if you say, that 'I am always a failure' then it is difficult to motivate yourself to do work if this negative thought is prevailing. No one is *always* a failure.

Words have power and if you are using powerful words to describe yourself and name yourself, then this can cause problems. 'I am a failure' can make it difficult for you to want to put the energy into your work. Another student once described to me how he didn't want to feel like a failure anymore. He was retaking exams. When I asked him about his exams he told me he got two As and one B. Yet to him he was a failure. I asked him what was a success to him and he said to be like his brother, who got As the first time he did the exams. He could never feel like he was a success or even enjoy the fact he had achieved good results.

Always Being Right

We are continually on trial to prove that our opinions and actions are correct. Being wrong is unthinkable and we will go to any length to demonstrate our 'rightness'. This can be very detrimental when it comes to studying. Part of the process of studying is to find out when you are wrong, so you can learn or you can improve. Students will avoid doing exams, practice tests or any way of testing themselves, because they want to be right or wish to avoid the pain of realising that they don't know the subject. Whereas the best thing they can do is attempt questions and look for feedback about where they were wrong and to learn from it.

I had a student who was upset that they had 'forgotten' so much. When I looked through their answers they had scored perfectly on two of the questions but on the third question they never knew the answer because they never learned it. They were willing to distort reality in a very negative way.

Targeting irrational thoughts using the ABCDE method

Ellis, who I previously mentioned, used an **ABCDE** system to teach the basics of CBT. Here are the five elements:

A = Activating event

B = Belief system

C = Emotional Consequences of A and B

D = Disputing irrational thoughts and beliefs.

E = Cognitive, Behavioural and Emotional effects of revised beliefs

A is the **activating event**. This is an event that triggers stress or worry. It might be a crisis in a personal relationship, a a poor grade, bad feedback or anything else.

B stands for **belief**. This tends to be whatever you believe about the particular event in A. If it is poor grades, then you could believe that you have no chance in the exams, and that you will not pass. You could believe that you are a failure.

C stands for the **consequences** of these irrational beliefs. Irrational thoughts produce bad consequences. They can be self-fulfilling prophecies. For example, if you expect to feel nervous and do poorly, you are setting yourself up to feel nervous and do poorly. Some people repeat negative thoughts again and again. This repetitive thinking is called rumination and it is a bit like self-programming. A person who is constantly thinking, 'This is horrible!' or some other irrational idea, may stay in a bad mood because of these thoughts.

D stands for **disputing** irrational beliefs. Ellis's treatment consists of challenging (disputing) a client's irrational beliefs as directly as possible. This is what you can do. You can test the validity of your own beliefs. This can be a simple as noticing how you've labelled yourself a failure. Is this true? Have you actually failed?

E stands for the **effects** of changing one's interpretation of a situation. If CBT is effective, a person loses their symptoms of anxiety or distress and sees a situation differently (some therapists call this *cognitive restructuring*). This means that you can now take practical action to solve the problems or have a less stressful reaction to situations.

So, how do you make this work for you? Now that you have read the list of potential irrational thoughts, you should reflect on whether you find yourself thinking this way. Once you are aware of how irrational thoughts are impinging on your study, it is time to use the ABCDE approach.

This is such a quick and simple task. Grab some paper and write it out. What do you believe, or what are you saying to yourself? what are the consequences of this? Next it is time to move on to disputing the belief. This simple exercise, of writing out and reflecting on your way of thinking, should help you to have a more favourable attitude. You should now be able to fix the problem, seek help or figure out what you need to do. In essence, you should feel a little better.

So, imagine that you have got a low grade in an exam (**Activating event**) you feel like you are a failure and that you will never get a good grade (**Belief**, in this instance it is a mix of errors in thinking, **Catastrophising** and **Labelling**). You get annoyed with yourself, you get angry with your teachers, you feel depressed and anxious. You then give up studying in the evening, avoid deadlines and get more stressed (these are the **Consequences** of this belief). If you take a moment and tackle these beliefs to see how real they are (**Dispute**) you may notice that you just misread a question and that is something that you can learn not to do again. You didn't fail every question, and you could have prepared a little earlier. This makes you feel a little better and gives you the focus to continue studying and more determination to not misread questions again (**Effectiveness** of your revised beliefs).

So many of the problems I have to tackle with students are the results of some irrational thoughts about what study is, or what they are capable of doing. Albert Ellis's approach is straightforward, quick and effective. In fact, he would hold open meetings demonstrating that the ABCDE approach worked. He did it every Friday night up until he died at the age of 93.

This approach works well in terms of exam anxiety and fear. A lot of students tend to have an emotion-focused approach to dealing with stress and this just makes things worse. This means targeting the emotional impact of stress which doesn't help when it comes to study. You can sit and moan about a problem, but that won't get the essay finished. CBT is more like a *problem-focused* way of coping. It looks at solutions to these problems and deals with them. However, if you are still feeling anxiety or that you could be depressed then it is important that you *seek professional help*.

Reducing stress through meditation

A popular and useful technique to reduce stress is to use meditation to help you to calm down and relax.

The idea behind this is that you use breathing exercises to create physiological calm. There are so many different ways to achieve this, and one even combines CBT and it is known as *mindful-based cognitive therapy.* I am not endorsing this or any other therapy, but it is worth checking out and seeing if it works for you.

A simple way to meditate is to just sit comfortably on a chair and **focus on breathing**. Make sure to turn off all electronic stuff, phones, computers, etc. How I use meditation is simple; you close your eyes, stay relaxed, and then you breath in and out. You then count the first in and out breath as one, the next is two, do this until you reach eight and start again. What you may notice is that your mind wanders, you might feel that this whole thing seems stupid. Don't think about it, just be aware that your mind is wandering over time you will get more used to this.

You will become better at this technique the more you do it. You can use your phone here if you want to, using the stopwatch to see how long you lasted. In the beginning, people usually last just a few minutes, but after regular meditation, it is possible to do this for much longer.

However, if you find that your mind is all over the place and you are thinking too much, rather than relaxing, then maybe a **guided meditation** is better. Look up versions of this with mantras and other techniques.

A simple one is to imagine you are **breathing in calm and letting go of stress** with every exhale. A psychological version of this is called mindfulness-based CBT. The purpose of all this is to calm you down. If you don't want to sit in a room meditating and feel a bit conspicuous, you can take a nice relaxing bath while you do this.

A final idea that is helpful when it comes to stress is to make sure you **do some exercise**. The simplest thing to do is take a walk, between study sessions. It could be to the shop or further. It does help.

SUMMARY

1 Sometimes stress can be a result of the demand that is placed on you, or how much you think you can control the amount of demand. This has a physiological response.

2 If you are prone to panic attacks or extreme anxiety to do with exams then you may need to seek professional help. Talk to your doctor and ask them for support.

3 A very good approach to deal with stress is Cognitive Behavioural Therapy (CBT).

1. Read through the list of errors in thinking and mark the ones that are most common for you.

2. Keep a diary for a few days of the thoughts you have in relation to stressful experiences.

3. It will only work if you apply the ABCDE method to the negative thoughts that you have. In the simplest form, you are testing the reality of the thoughts.

4. It might be worth going back over your goals so that you have a clear outline of what you need to do in order to succeed. At least then you can see if you are on target and you can actually enjoy some breaks in your study.

5. Try meditation, exercise or just taking a bath to see if that helps to relax you.

6. Talk over your worries with someone, but do come up with some practical solutions to your problems.

7 Revision

You have probably used the word *revision* many, many times. Revision is going over the material again, it is *not* doing it for the first time. You have to have learned something in order to revise it. Everything I have mentioned in the previous chapters is important: **time management** helps you with the best use of your time in revision. **Goals** help you to realise what you need to do and to motivate you on how to do it. The **PQRR technique** helps to create better notes to revise from and the idea of making **creative revision tools** help you revise and test yourself.

It is important that you **test yourself regularly** prior to exams. Don't let a day of revision go by without testing yourself. This is how you can find out what you know and what you don't know. You don't have to spend hours writing out essays, you can do skeletal answers or plans. You can bullet point a plan for every possible extended or essay question in one sitting for some subjects. The important thing is that you get into a habit of doing this. You should know what is expected of you in the exam. You need to plan what it is you're going to revise. Use past papers to guide you and always find the specification to be sure everything is covered. It is never too early to start revising. Once you have learned something and covered the material, then it is time to revise it.

Study space

You need to make sure you **work in the correct environment**. *Not* in front of the TV. Music can sometimes be OK, but you need to find the right kind. It's got to be something that's just there in the background, that you're not thinking about at all. Music without singing is better as it's less distracting.

A clean environment to study is preferable but don't worry too much about obsessively tidying your study area. It does matter a little because mess can be stressful, but if that is your only problem when it comes to revision then that's great. What *is* vital, however, is that the place you are studying is actually fit for study. If you have a bag filled with crumpled paper and half written notes, then you need to sort this out using the time management and note-keeping methods mentioned in previous chapters.

If your family are intrusive and disturb your study then find somewhere where you can actually work. The library is ideal but if it is a noisy place, as unfortunately many school libraries can be, then **find somewhere quiet where you can study**. These may seem like minor things but you need to reduce anything that will cause you stress and/or distract you during revision time.

Check your notes

Make sure your notes are understandable. This is all mentioned in the PQRR method, but it is advisable that you check that your notes make sense and that you aren't missing any key information. Often students start something, decide to work on it later, only to forget about it. You need to check that your notes are complete and that they actually make sense. This is something I advise that people do as they go along.

Three stages of revision

It is easy to break revision down into three stages, I adapted this from a revision guide I used many years ago as I found it to be really useful.

Stage 1 – Understand. Most students only get partly through this and technically this is the precursor to revision. You need to study the topic slowly; make sure you understand the important concepts. I know that I mentioned this a few times but **use the PQRR technique** to have an overview and understanding of the material.

Stage 2 – Summarise and memorise. You can use the PQRR technique. You can then summarise the material again. This becomes even more useful nearer the exams as you may not have covered some of the material in months.

Try a few creative ways to study, e.g. mind maps,

mnemonics, skeletal plans, making flash cards. Spend 25 minutes learning the material you have got notes on, then take a five minute break. Then test yourself on what you have covered.

Stage 3 – Track and review. This is simple. Use a big sheet of paper (A3) to write down the revision you have done for each subject. What I suggest is that you use a sheet for each subject and divide it into sections. This allows you to see that you have distributed your time equally among your subjects. You can then alter your revision goals. As time moves on, you will need to adjust your revision plans. Students often try to stick rigidly to their goal but may need to adjust and alter what they are doing. If you are becoming stuck on topics, then seek help for the topics you don't understand. Again, test yourself on the topics you have revised to see what you need to cover again. This is the best way to approach revision. It is best to start revision as soon as you have done a topic and then revise it again before the exams.

Parents, friends and partners

There are many people around you who want to support you. It is important that you don't feel like they're getting in the way, but instead find a way to work with them to help you study. You can use them as a soundboard to test out how you know the information. It is best that you get them to test you with flashcards, or past exam papers. Get them to make flashcards with you. They can be your allies. Give them your phone to look after while you're studying or discuss with them ways of restricting your access to social media, if you're finding it hard to do this on your own. By including them, they are less likely to cause you stress, and it is you who has chosen to do this.

No success without effort

Students have this idea that some people are naturally good at study and it is about ability. This has been proven to be untrue. Carol Dweck has looked at this in great detail. She has written a book called *Mindset* and it deals with her research into this. She divided into groups those who believed that success was about ability, who she said have a *fixed mindset*, and those that believe it is about effort, believed to have a *growth mindset*. She has investigated the effects of these mindsets and it is quite amazing.

When people with a fixed mindset encounter problems they are more likely to give up. She would take a single child out of the classroom for a nonverbal IQ test consisting of a series of puzzles – puzzles easy enough that all the children would do fairly well. Once the child finished the test, the researchers told each student their score, then gave them a single line of praise. Randomly divided into groups, some were praised for their intelligence. They were told, 'You must be smart at this.' Other students were praised for their effort: 'You must have worked really hard'; the students in the effort group. By developing this *growth mindset* (persisting, working at improving and believing that success can come through effort rather than be the result of 'natural' intelligence), the students, according to Dweck, learn more actively and with a higher degree of free will, making for more autonomous learners.

This is important because if you think succeeding in something is more about *ability,* then you need to change this to thinking about *effort.* I ask my students if they believe that success is about ability or effort. The ones that think it is about ability find it difficult to believe it is actually about effort. A better way of thinking about it is; some people may be better at some things than you, you may need to put in more effort than they do. You need to put the effort in anyway, you need to work harder and more effectively. And if you're getting 100% in every subject without any work, that's great, but you won't be reading this book.

The truth is that success in subjects comes from work. How *much* work is best figured out by your grades. If you are struggling then you have to work harder or more effectively. If you move away from thinking about it being ability, you are more likely to become more successful because you will start to work on time management, goals and active study.

It is amazing how little some students put into study.

They have lots of excuses and other things that they need to be doing. Their lives mimic the lives of rockstars, rather than that of students. The truth is you have a job to do, and that is *to be a student*. If you want to be a good/excellent student, then do the work. If you take weekends off and do very little work, coupled with missing lessons and partying hard, how do you expect to get the best grades?

Dr. Anders Ericsson has done research on expertise and he suggests that to be an expert at something, you need to put 10,000 hours of practice in. I am not suggesting that is what you need to do for your study. I am suggesting that you should realise that the more effort, the more work and the more exam practice you do, the better your results will be.

If you look at the biographies of people whom you consider successful, you will find that they generally put in a lot of hard work and effort.

Bad teaching and lack of support

The terrible truth is that there are teachers who are not very good and they can cause you to lose grades or even misguide you. I think this is terrible and I hate to hear the stories of students who avoid working due to the lack of support and bad teaching. I will never condone bad teaching but you need to move away from blame and toward taking control. You need to develop skills to help you in higher education and the workplace. There is no requirement for university professors to hand hold and support you; this is something that teachers in secondary education should be doing properly. The earlier you learn to work independently and effectively the better your academic career will be.

I speak to outstanding teachers all the time, they follow the syllabus and cover the material and their students do well. They sometimes get complaints when the students just want someone to blame. I have also seen the negative effects of bad teaching, which include poor grades, retaking an entire year and missing opportunities. I have a thing I tell my students, it is **'trust but verify'**. Trust that I am guiding you correctly, but always check to see that I am. I never get offended when a student highlights a problem and I don't mind students grabbing the syllabus or checking the book. Most times I have been correct but teachers can make mistakes. It is vital that you **take control of the workload**. The most important thing is that you understand what is expected of you in the exams and that the material has been covered. By taking control you can remedy problems earlier and not be disadvantaged. This control will reduce your stress.

Check the specification material

The first point of protection for you is to **make sure you have a course outline or syllabus** and you are aware of what the exam board expects from you.

Download all the papers and check that the materials you are getting are relevant. If you are worried, take a moment to talk to the teacher. If they are not responsive then I advise you make a clear and reasonable complaint about your concerns.

Coursework is your responsibility

I work with students who have failed their subjects and sometimes they blame the teacher, when it might have been down to them. They might have wanted more than the teacher can actually offer or had unreasonable expectations. This seems to pop up a lot in coursework, where the onus to produce the work is on the student. Make sure to use goals and planning strategies when producing coursework. Factor in time for a draft earlier than you need to so that you can get good feedback. Make the changes and give it your best.

Staying healthy

It is important that you **take care of your health and eat properly**. I always include this here because students like to go out in the evenings, go to parties and stay out late. I like to say to students to avoid this during revision. You could potentially lose days of studying. If it is too big a sacrifice to give up parties, meeting friends and drinking then this is a problem that you need to address. This period of study is a short time in your life and if you want to do well in your exams, then you will need to take them seriously. You can't work productively if you are too tired and/or hungry. By staying healthy you can avoid becoming ill at a time when you need to be at your best.

Sleeping habits

I have terrible sleeping habits and I really do feel it when I have been up late watching movies or TV. The fact is, many of us don't have healthy sleep patterns. So just ask yourself, do you feel tired throughout the day regularly? Does your tiredness interfere with your study or work? Many students live in a state of constant sleep deprivation. This can have major knock-on effects. It means that they need to nap, sleep in, or they have difficulty concentrating. If you are sleep deprived during exams it can make you more likely to make avoidable mistakes when you're sitting them.

So what *shouldn't* you do if you are having problems sleeping?

1. It is not a great idea to listen to music just before you go to sleep.
2. If you are sensitive to caffeine then it's advisable not to drink it before you go to bed.
3. If you like watching movies before you go to bed, then organise this beforehand, look at the length of the movie, or the episodes of the TV series. Shows tend to be structured with cliffhangers, leaving you wanting more if it is a good show. So, you'll need to us a little willpower not to binge on shows till really late at night.

4. sleeping in till really late just sets your body clock at unusual times. If you want to lay in then it has to be planned.
5. If you work best at night then work at night as I have mentioned.
6. Another surprising thing is that if you exercise during the day, it can make you tired enough to sleep well at night. However, if you exercise too late at night it can wake you up mentally as it is stimulating and, while tired, you may feel more awake.
7. Alcohol consumption does interfere with your sleep. So if you are drinking and going out then do expect to feel bad, lose sleep and have hangovers. As I've said before, be honest with yourself about what your priorities are during your study.

All of this can be avoided. For some, however, it may be something more. If you are having ongoing sleep problems, it is worth talking to your doctor. If worry is keeping you up late at night, worry about exams or your workload, please look back at the stress chapter and use some of the techniques there. Again, talk to your doctor about this if you feel you need to.

SUMMARY

1 Review the strategies in **Chapter 2 Time management**.

2 Revision can be done using three steps, first you seek to get an understanding, then you memorise and then you review.

3 The best way to review is to sit and test yourself.

4 Try to get your friends and family on your side.

5 The truth about success in study is that it's about effort.

6 Don't allow poor support by teachers or bad teaching stop you from getting a grade. It is *your* grade so you must become responsible for making sure you have everything you need.

7 If you are having problems with sleep then make sure that you seek help or try to get into better sleeping habits. Don't have a lot of screen time just before you go to sleep. Exercise during the day and avoid alcohol.

8 Exams

These are just a few, brief, techniques to help you during the exam period. Hopefully you've enjoyed the subjects you have been studying and recognise the benefit of learning purely for the sake of learning, but from a qualification perspective, the exam is the end point of your study and the chance to demonstrate what you've learnt. You want to make sure that you give yourself every opportunity to perform at your best in every exam during this period.

Before the exam

The night before the exam, it is important that you **get a good night's sleep**. Don't go out with your friends or spend hours on the internet, however much you might think it will reduce stress. You may be anxious and worried prior to the exam, so try to relax. If you work too hard early on before the exams start and exhaust yourself, it will have a detrimental effect at the end of the exams and this could be damaging and your impact your overall grade.

Ideally, you should go for steady and well-planned revision and **avoid cramming** for the exam. Cramming, which is leaving everything to the last moment, is reported by many students to be a great way of passing exams, but it is less and less effective the higher your qualifications. Maybe you got away with it during your GCSEs but this is no benchmark for the level of depth required for an A level. Cramming is the act of a desperate person; it creates panic. So don't leave it until the last moment. It can undo a lot of the good work you have done to date.

It is a good idea to **try not to panic**, or be near those that do panic. If you are feeling panicked, recognise the process your body is going through, put things in perspective and run through some of the stress-reducing methods mentioned in Chapter 6. If you have friends who panic, tell them you are studying or that you have exams. If they persist in pestering and panicking you, then definitely ask them for some space. However, do be a little gentle with others around exam time, they may be struggling too. If someone else is really struggling, you are better encouraging them to seek help from a professional, as you may not have the training to help them.

Get up early on the day of the exam, and avoid rushing to the exam or being late.

Eat something for breakfast. Apart from the usual reasons why it is important, it can be distracting for you and others to have your stomach rumbling during the exam. Go for something which releases energy slowly rather than a quick burst of energy from something sugary. Avoid energy drinks (you should always avoid energy drinks, but especially during exams).

Arrive at the exam hall in good time. Make sure not to put yourself in any situations which might mean you arrive just before the exam begins. But if this does happen, don't panic. It helps to arrive early but it won't be the deciding factor in how well you do.

Avoid looking through your notes directly before the exam. This is usually seen in the manic page-flicking students do prior to being called into the exam. You should know the information by now. Looking through your books at the last minute is likely to make it harder for you to recall everything you need to answer every question. If you are the type of person who is overly anxious prior to exams then follow the advice in the stress section, or talk to some professionals.

The exam

Now for the exam stuff. As a teacher and an examiner, I have seen the consequences of bad exam technique. Most can be avoided really easily. If you have made these mistakes in the past then learn from them.

During the exam it is important that you **read the questions carefully**. Far too many times students have failed and then had to resit an exam because they misread questions. This is terrible and this is easily avoided. Take a breath and then do the next thing I suggest – it really helps.

Plan the responses and stick to the plan. This is

so important. A plan only needs to be a couple of minutes of your time, a few words or themes written down quickly – use spare paper. Then take a quick look at the question and make sure you have read it correctly. I would never write an essay without a plan. I once marked down during a month of revision how many times I said 'plan your essays' to a class. It was 43. One of the students who got a B – she tended to ramble or run out of time in exams – bought me a mug with 'Always plan your essays' on it. I asked her if she planned hers and she said 'no, I was too busy'. I wonder if she could have got an A if she did.

In the exam, **only focus on your own behaviour**. Do not look around at others and what they are doing. It is what *you* should be doing that counts. Don't look over at another student who is writing and writing pages of information and think 'I am going to fail', you are using valuable exam time being distracted.

During the exam it is good to **underline key words** where appropriate.

This next point is vital – you must be very **aware of your timing** in the exams. I ask students to raise their hand if they ran out of time in the exam. When they have raised their hand I tell them that they did not *run out* of time, they *mismanaged* their time. Far too often people mismanage their time in the exams. If you practise exam skills beforehand and get used to how much you should be writing then this will help in the exam. If you have an hour to do an exam and there are 60 marks then you have a minute per mark (if only it was that easy, but to be honest it isn't hard). If the exam is an hour and a half and you have three questions to do then it is half an hour a question. Students can lose valuable marks and therefore grades by not paying attention to this. Don't let this be you.

If you finish, **go over your questions**; never, ever, ever leave early! This sounds obvious and for some it is unlikely that you would. I once had a student who left an hour and a half exam with three essay questions after an hour. When I ran into him he assured me that he had nailed it definitely got the A. Months later, when the results were in, it was revealed that he got a D.

According to my former professor Aidan Moran, people fail exams because:

1. They did not prepare enough.
2. They did not read the questions correctly.
3. They left answers blank or too short.
4. They failed to answer the question they were asked or they failed to do all the parts that they were asked to do.
5. They were guilty of unnecessary repetition – usually the fault of poorly planned answers.
6. They failed to use their time efficiently, which usually means they ran out of time.
7. There was poor presentation of work, with sloppy, rambling sentences or no paragraphs.
8. They finished before the exam was over.

I would add to this list a few more reasons why people fail:

1. Not learning from past mistakes. This means that they go on to make the same mistakes again. If, for instance, cutting corners and not practicing exam questions caused you to get poor grades, then learn from this. This is the sad part of teaching and marking; seeing how close a student could get to success if only they had tried a little more or learned from their mistakes.

2. Ignoring the feedback that has been given throughout the year. Look at recurring themes of your feedback and try to find solutions to them.

3. Trying to take risks with what material gets covered in the hope of reducing the amount of work that needs to be done. This is relying on you or your teacher having a sound system of prediction. Sometimes it works, but can you take the risk of it not working and then failing? You should cover everything properly. Sometimes a lecturer will give hints – this is different. Trying to guess what is coming up is dangerous, my advice is not to do it.

If any of these ring true for you then now, before the exam is sat, is time to fix them.

What if your mind goes blank? This is a terrifying experience. A simple suggestion is to **move on to**

another question and then come back, but you *must* come back. It may be worth brainstorming when you return to the question. If you still have difficulties with the question, do not panic, do some visualisation techniques as this can trigger your memories. If you covered the question, think about the page in the book, imagine what your teacher said. Start jotting down a plan. These words should act as cues for you to remember. If you have been using the PQRR method, and testing yourself, then this will reduce the likelihood of it happening. But it can happen. The key is to not get stressed as you may create more problems. Take a deep breath and read the question again and try the techniques just mentioned. It is advisable not to leave the answer blank, just **attempt the question**.

Oh, and **Good Luck**. The golfer Gary Player once said, 'the harder you work, the luckier you get'.

SUMMARY

1 Get rest just before the exams start.

2 Don't panic, and don't be around those that will cause you panic.

3 Read the questions carefully.

4 Plan your answers.

5 Make sure your writing is legible.

6 Use your time effectively in exams, be aware of how much time you actually have per question.

7 If your mind goes blank during the exam questions, then take a moment, possibly move to another question, brainstorm and stay calm.

Bibliography

Time management

Gillian Butler, Tony Hope, *Managing your mind: The Mental Fitness Guide* (OUP, 2007)

Kenneth Goldsmith, *Wasting Time on the Internet* (Harper Collins, 2016)

Caroline Buchanan, *The 15 Minute Rule: How to stop procrastinating and take charge of your life* (Robinson, 2012)

Francesco Cirillo, *The Pomodoro Technique: The Acclaimed Time-Management System That Has Transformed How We Work* (Currency, 2018)

Elaine Payne, Lesley Whitaker, *Developing Essential Study Skills* (FT/Prentice Hall, 2006)

Andrew Northedge, *The Good Study Guide* (Open University, 2005)

Goals

Peter Drucker, *The Practice of Management* (Heinemann, 1955)

George Doran, *"S.M.A.R.T. Goals", American Management Association Review* (November 1981)

Victor Frankl, *Man's Search for Meaning* (Rider, 2004)

Making good notes

Aidan Moran, *Managing Your Own Learning at University: A Practical Guide* (University College Dublin Press, 2000)

Bransford, Johnson, 'Contextual prerequisites for understanding:

Some investigations of comprehension and recall', *Journal of Verbal Learning & Verbal Behavior* (1972)

Creative study activities

Tony Buzan, *The Mind Map Book* (BBC Active, 2009)

Dealing with stress

Rhena Branch, *Cognitive Behavioural Therapy for Dummies.* For Dummies (2010)

Revision

Carol Dweck, *Mindset: How you can fulfil your potential.* Robinson (2012)

K.A, Ericsson, R, Krampe and C. Tesch-Romer. *The role of deliberate practice in the acquisition of expert performance. Psychological Review, 100* (1993)

Exams

Mike Evans, *How to pass your exams* (How To books, 2010)

Acknowledgements

I want to thank Adam Dale. Without him, this would still be on my computer, and Yasmine, whose first edit of the book made it possible. Professor Aidan Moran from UCD who instilled in me the desire to learn about study skills. Through his books and teachings I was able to go and help many students in the UK. My wife and daughter, I do these things for them and with them. All the people who have taken a chance on me teaching study skills in the establishments I have worked. Ralph Dennison, Joel Roderick, the late Chris Mathieson, Mario Peters and Rafi Peters, Fiona Pocock, Mark Love, Carol Nyssen, Feras Al Zudi and Roy Carrington. I had the desire to teach these topics and they all allowed me to do it, as a result I now have a book. Andrew Hogan who has been one of the best supports in all my endeavours, I trust his advice and support without which I couldn't imagine. All my friends and colleagues who have listened to me and sent students to me for help. Zoe Lundy, she was instrumental in the creation of a yet to be published book that was the source for this one. Adrian Budd, Sean Murphy (still owes me for the bet), Magnus Moar, Rachel Waring, Paula Chorlton, Michael Collins, James Platt, Ed Horn, Lamine Djellali, Nick Parkin, Kathryn Aveyard, Brendon Connelly, Kevin Dillow, Tamar Maclellan, Rob Harris, Sinead Garry, Sian Harris, Louise Walker, Andy McGuffie, Jenny Wells, and Ian Nixon. I want to thank my family all of them, My Mom and my sisters who helped me through the exams by being extra supportive, Delia, Sylvia and Trisha. Regina and Graham who have encouraged me and listened to all my ideas.

All the students I have taught who have been Guinea pigs in some of the stuff I do, they responded so well. Iona Brown, Callum McDonald, Rory Stoddard, Robbie Wood, Will Henwood, The Broadribb sisters, Ali Franklin, Jake Parker, Fabian (Scandy), Valeria Shunina, Constantin Wosalla, Victor, Seb Rocca, Seb Ford, Robert Blakey, Lina Seidleitz, Nadia Anya Walker, Michael Lee (Micheala), Maia Louise Sherratt, Ivan Lopatin, Peter Ussher, Marcus Naschke. Kira, Rahil Habibli, Wanyu, Claudia, Zhora

Jenkinson Simon and Charlotte Deeves, Adam Deeves, Luvena Leung, Ezra Chen, Luke Mooney, Edel Mooney, Cressida Lawlor, Clara Murray, Theresa Garfield, Helen Hines, Askar Keen, Andrew Oglivy, Alexander Kulakov, Rachael Nyssen, Denis Deady, Joe O' Regan, Hugh Sheridan, Adrian Mongan, and everyone else who has given me the support I needed to get where I needed to be. The students who reminded me of why I do what I do, Ines and Sophie for reminding me what works. For all the students I have yet to teach, the ones I will make buy this book. Hopefully will mention them in the next one.

Printed in Great Britain
by Amazon

40197401R00066